Cinderella with Wrong Shoes

Dear Hannah & Virginia,
 I'm glad we are friends. Please continue to be friendly & enjoy this book.
  JEN & Au̵̶̶̶

Cinderella with Wrong Shoes

Poems by a young woman with autism

Jennifer Fan & Autumn Fan

Writer's Showcase
San Jose New York Lincoln Shanghai

Cinderella with Wrong Shoes
Poems by a young woman with autism

All Rights Reserved © 2001 by Jennifer Fan and Autumn Fan

No part of this book may be reproduced or transmitted in any form or by any means, graphic, electronic, or mechanical, including photocopying, recording, taping, or by any information storage retrieval system, without the permission in writing from the publisher.

Writer's Showcase
an imprint of iUniverse, Inc.

For information address:
iUniverse, Inc.
5220 S. 16th St., Suite 200
Lincoln, NE 68512
www.iuniverse.com

ISBN: 0-595-21105-4

Printed in the United States of America

Content

Illness, Struggle, and Hope 1
    A Brighter Tomorrow 3
    Mom, What's Wrong with Me? 4
    Schizophrenia and Faith in God 5
    I'm A Lazy Poet 6
    Two Big Eyes 7
    I'm Different 8
    I'm Always Tired and Sleepy 9
    I Can't Sit Still and Concentrate 11
    Lazy, Sleepy but Happy 12
    I Don't Remember 13
    I'm a Cat with Nine Lives 14
    We're Not Alone 15
    Not Worth a Scream 16
    Meeting with Dr. Gerhardt 17
    Adult Autism 18
    Perhaps 19
    Sneaky Me 20
    Watch My Weight 21
    Looking at the Light 22
    I'm no Longer Afraid 23
    Mom is Thinking about Dropping Courses 24
    Break Free 25
    I'm a Unique Person not Like Anyone Else 26
    Priority Has Changed 27

Cinderella with Wrong Shoes

Growing Pain 29
   A Weird Dream 31
   If You Let Her Come In 32
   What to Do? What Shall I Do? 34
   Everybody is Working but Me 35
   Simplicity 36
   Inseparable 38
   Meow, Meow, Meow 40
   A Good-Looking Man 41
   It Has Been Coming Along 42
   A Hang-Out 43
   I See, Then I See 44
   I Won't Do It Again 45
   If I were a Twin 47
   We Want, We Don't Want 48
   Slow Down 49
   We're on Our Own 50
   I Wish He Was Single 51
   Cinderella with Wrong Shoes 52

Nature and Animals 53
   Holy Clouds 55
   A Divine Secret 56
   Sunbathing 57
   The Life of Riverside 58
   Thunder or Fireworks 59
   Fire Rain 60
   The Plant is Gone 61
   Please Open Up 63
   Everything is Beautiful 64
   Rain 65

The Whole Town is So Quiet 66
Summer Outdoor Concert 67
A Piece of Memory 68
It is All Right 70
A Romantic Thing 71
A Beautiful Afternoon 73
Thanks for Keeping Up the Beautiful Backyards 74
Guess Who Am I? 75
A Dragonfly 76
A New Friend Visits Me 77
A Dog and A Little Girl 78
Stay Happily Ever After 79
I Hope You Didn't Get Hurt 80
Wishes For Kittens 81
Crows Everywhere 83
The Fish 85

Family 87
Last Me the Whole Life Long 89
Grandpa, Have a Nice Trip 91
With God, Nothing is Too Hard 92
Sing 93
Grandpa Squeezed Me 95
He is My Father 96
A Strong Lady 98
The Way 100
Swing Straight, Swing Out 101
Funny Mom 103
Must Be the Wind 104
You Are Cold 105
I Love My Sister 106

A Belated Birthday Gift 108
   Slow Down Sister, I Can't Keep up 109
   A Star or a Doll 110

Friends 113
   A Long Time Ago 115
   She is Not My Mom 116
   A Heavenly Thing 117
   God's Love Flourishes 118
   He Will Lead Us to His Door 120
   Danica Isn't Feeling Well 121
   Passionate Friendship 122
   Barbara Livingston 123
   A Surprise Gift 125
   Louisa 127
   She is a Dance Teacher, Not a Science Teacher 128
   Mother and Son 129
   For the Unselfish Reason We Let Go 130
   A Special Friend 132
   Mr. Wu's Hope and Joy 134
   A Girl As Quiet As Me 136
   I Look and Look 137
   My Friend Went to France 138
   Chinese Calligraphy 139
   Kevin, the Next-Door Neighbor's Boy 140

Travel 141
   Holy Spirit Helps Me 143
   Night Sky 145
   Identity 147
   A Scenario is Playing Out 149

 A Bus Ride 150
 Misbehavior 151
 A Good American 152
 Queen Latifah Show 153
 A Special Gift from New York City 154
 How can New York City Treat Us This Way? 155
 Dream Trip is About to Come True 156
 Blizzard of 2000 158

Every Day Life 159
 A Lonesome Poet 161
 Please Come 162
 Two Dollars 163
 Flat Tire 165
 Without A Doubt 166
 Nothing Much Nothing Big 167
 Get Out and Use Your Feet 168
 Noisy Chair 169
 Autumn Terrace 170
 You Have Nothing On 171
 Reliving The Wars 172
 Left Hand too 173
 Dad is Home 174
 The House of Coffee 175
 Seven Hills of Istanbul 176
 A New Diner 177
 The Whole Place is Ours 179
 Kids Everywhere 181
 Today, Today, Today 183
 Didn't I Know Him 184
 No Money, No Honey 186

Appendix- Depression 187
    A Scapegoat 189
    I Don't Deserve to Live 190
    I've Missed Out a Lot of Things 191
    I am Fidgety 192
    Hair 193
    Bye-Bye Right Hand 194
    I am a Ghost 195
    What is It About Being Beautiful? 196
    Sex, Sexy 197
    Being Ill 198
    A Knife 199
    A Rock 200
    Who is Myself? 201
    I'm Left at a Grave Site 202

Foreword

by Autumn Fan

When any child is classified as learning disabled, it deeply affects that child, the family, and the child's educators. The cause of the disability is broad. It involves complicated physical, mental and emotional issues.

My daughter Jennifer was diagnosed as learning disabled at the age of eight. As her mother, I had an extremely hard time adapting to the concept that my daughter had a learning handicap, especially since my first daughter, Jessie, was a gifted student. I was not prepared to face the challenge of a child with special needs.

When Jennifer was in the second grade, the school notified me that Jennifer was experiencing a hard time; she was not able to keep up with the learning pace of others in her class. After a conference with school officials and the teacher, Jennifer was placed in a special program along with other learning disabled students. She remained in that program throughout her school years.

Even though it was difficult for me to accept what was happening, I had to admit that Jennifer had shown signs of difficulties earlier. She didn't speak until she was two; she didn't call out for Dad or Mom. If she needed something, she would point to the object instead of saying it. Besides, she played by herself without bothering anyone in the house most of the time.

At age three, Jennifer underwent a hearing test and had surgery to put a tube in her left ear. We hired a speech therapist who taught Jennifer phrases, and a few simple sentences in two years. Her condition had improved, but only slightly. Jennifer was still shy and quiet. She avoided participating in activities with other children by saying that she was tired. She was a shy, quiet and well-behaved little girl.

Cinderella with Wrong Shoes

My husband and I were hoping that someday she would outgrow her shyness and eventually make up for whatever she had missed. After all, each child has his or her own learning pattern and pace.

When Jennifer graduated from high school in 1996, she continued her education at a local community college. I decided to go with her in hopes of assisting her in any way I could. It was a difficult task. Jennifer had an extremely hard time memorizing. Although she understood most of the materials, she couldn't organize her thoughts to write them down on paper. I summarized and repeated everything with her again and again. It required special patience. Sometimes, I lost my temper due to deadlines for assignments and exams. Other times, I simply cried because I was frustrated. Jennifer cried with me at times because it was hard for her to see me suffer in this way.

In April of 2000, after a lingering flu, Jen entered a major depression. She heard voices and saw things that were not there. She became suicidal and paranoid. For three weeks she was in and out of the psychiatric ward of the hospital—it was the most harrowing three weeks our family had ever experienced. Follow up visits with her psychiatrist revealed that Jennifer had been suffering from autism.

The news didn't shock me too much. I had suspected she was autistic for a long time. The reason I didn't pursue it was because I thought an autistic person wouldn't be able to communicate and show his or her affection. Jennifer had shown a special passion for animals and was able to demonstrate her compassion for other people in her daily activities such as church, home and school.

It was only later that I learned that autism is a neurological disorder which involves a wide spectrum of characteristics. Those who share many of the same characteristics of classical autism, yet with average or above-average intelligence are classified as having Asperger's disorder or high functioning autism.

Asperger's disorder was first described by an Austrian physician named Hans Asperger at about the same time as autism but not officially named as a diagnosis by the American Psychiatric Association until 1994. Generally speaking, many Asperger sufferers have a hard time in social interaction. They also show difficulties in planning and coping with change. Their stress from facing the complexity of daily life often leads them to depression as a result.

Presently, Jen is undergoing more neuropsychological tests in order to further pinpoint underlying problems. Despite the difficulties she has been through, Jennifer is a jewel in our family. She is kind, pure and gentle. She is definitely a special gift from God. Whatever we have experienced or will face in the future, we thank the Lord for her. For He created her; He made us learn and grow through this child.

I also want to give special thanks to Dr. Shin, the psychiatrist. He encouraged Jennifer to write a daily journal. Instead of writing journal entries, I have been helping her to put all her thoughts, feelings, observations and gratitude in poems. There is a Chinese saying, "When you come upon the mountain, go around it." Maybe hurdles in life never go away, but changing our perspective toward the problems may help us to overcome and reach beyond.

Acknowledgements

I would like to express my gratitude for the people who helped to make my dream of publishing this book a reality.

My sister Jessie encouraged me to put together all the poems into a book; Sharline, my childhood friend, helped to edit my poems. The entire staff of writing lab at Brookdale Community College who proofread the poem; Johnny, my cousin, who set up a beautiful website exclusively for me. Of course, I would like to thank my mom for co-authoring the book with me; my dad for providing me with financial help.

I also would like to thank On-Ching and Daisy Yue, Pastor Al McNally, his wife Ruth, Pastor Paul Chang, his wife Carol, Sheauling Tang, Lisa, Vandy and Danica Lee who were among the first to come to my aid when I was ill.

My sincere thanks for all the medical help from my doctors, Dr. Shin, Dr. Rutan, Dr. Ilaria and Dr. Chen.

Most of all I would give all the glory to God. He provides me with all the kind people and the support I need.

Jennifer Fan

Illness, Struggle, and Hope

A Brighter Tomorrow

I bought a bottle of champagne to celebrate.
"Celebrate what?" You may ask.
"Life," I reply.

I bought a bottle of champagne to taste.
"Taste what?" You may wonder.
"Life", again I reply.

Champagne sparkles.
Champagne has a tiny bit of bitterness
When swallowed.

Our lives are like that.
Many struggles lead to sparkle.

When we taste it and swallow,
We are guaranteed
To celebrate a brighter tomorrow.

7-4-2000

Mom, What's Wrong with Me?

"Mom, what's wrong with me?"
I asked, when we sat in the car.

"Nobody knows, I guess,"
I answered myself
When I sensed the quietness.

"Honey, I think you have a mild case of autism.
It's not your fault."

I'm not surprised.
Lately, Mom has been reading a lot
About autism.

"I think I have a little bit of schizophrenia too,"
I said.

Mom looked at me and said,
"Honey, no matter what it is,
We will trust the Lord and stick together."

7-4-2000

Schizophrenia and Faith in God

"Mom, schizophrenia hits people in their twenties,"
I said to Mom as we were having our routine promenade
Around the neighborhood.

Mom was a little startled.
She responded,
"Where did you learn that from?"

"From the Internet at school a while ago."

Mom fell into silence.
A split second later, she replied,
"Jen, is that what you really think you have?
You were pretty shaken up, weren't you?"

I nodded.
At least Mom understood.

"Have you also learned about cures?" Mom added.
"I guess not. I don't remember," I answered.

"Jen, I'm not sure you have schizophrenia.
Still whatever it is, we can work on prevention can't we?"

I nodded.

Both Mom and I decided on:
Reducing stress.
Keeping up with medication.
Having daily faith in God.

7-15-2000

I'm A Lazy Poet

I'm a lazy poet.
Million of poems in my heart
I've just had to postpone them.

Sorry poems
I don't know what my problem is.
I need another poet
To extract my poems.

I have one in my home.
She is my mom who writes Chinese poems.
To me, she blew the horn.
She said, "Don't waste your poems."

I'm sorry, dear poems,
I'm a lazy poet.

7-4-2000

Two Big Eyes

Two googly eyes look at me
From a stroller.
It is a little baby boy.
A year old, maybe.

I used to look like that.
Two googly eyes.
Mother's friends used to call me
E.T. eyes.

One day
Mom left me on a countertop
In a bank nearby.
I didn't cry.
I didn't even try.
I watched her with my two big eyes,
From behind.

I don't talk much in my life.
Nor do I cry.
My two big eyes,
They don't hide.

7-5-2000

I'm Different

Yellow school buses are coming out
From the YMCA Arrowhead campsite in Marlboro;
It's summer camp time for children.

I've never attended a summer camp in my life;
Not that I missed out or anything, just that I'm different.

I admire those kids who have all the energy within;
I don't have that.

Mom often picked me up at the teacher's request
On school field days.
For I didn't want to participate,
Only wanted to idle away the whole day.

Although Mom searched for summer camp opportunities;
She couldn't stand the possibility
That I might drown or get into an accident of any kind.
For my mind wasn't there with the crowd.

I didn't miss summer camp or anything;
I'm just different.

7-11-2000

I'm Always Tired and Sleepy

I don't know what it is.
I'm always tired and sleepy.

Luckily,
I have a very comfortable bed;
Lying here I get to enjoy all the sunlight. Not bad.
The harmonies of wonderful nature also float in.

I hear gentle rain touching the ground.
Soft wind dancing around.
Birds, dogs and cats surround me.
Be very quiet.
They're singing, barking and meowing.
Above, I hear airplanes and helicopters fly by.
They are all the wonderful nature friends of mine.

I don't know what it is;
I'm always tired and sleepy.
When I attend activities,
I usually end up
Sitting in the corner, all alone.

I was there in many places:
Dancing schools, Chinese school,
Piano lessons and birthday parties,
But you hardly saw me
For I was invisible.

People may think
I'm lazy, spoiled or being overprotected.
Whatever it is,
I'm always tired and sleepy.

Only my wonderful nature friends,
Are able to heal me.

7-12-2000

I Can't Sit Still and Concentrate

I can't sit still and concentrate.
I couldn't do it before,
And I can't do it now.

I know
It can be annoying;
When you want my attention.

But, I can't help it,
I just can't sit still and pay attention.
I couldn't do it before,
And I can't do it now.

My mind goes out.
My eyes go about.
And I get millions of excuses for
Not wanting to sit still.

I get up
To get myself a cup of water,
To take a shower,
To get mail,
To wash my hands.
You name it.

I just can't sit still and concentrate.
I couldn't do it before
And I can't do it now.

7-18-2000

Lazy, Sleepy but Happy

You must think it is a strange combination:
Lazy, sleepy but happy.
It is me.
As long as you don't ask too much from me,
I'm happy.

I don't answer your questions
For I'm lazy.
It is me.
If you let me sleep all I need,
I'm happy.

Don't drive me crazy.
I'm lazy, sleepy, but happy.
Try to understand me.

7-15-2000

I Don't Remember

People always ask,
"What did you do?"

"I don't remember,"
Is what they get from me.

I'm not joking.
I really don't remember
What I just did today
Or the day before.

Here we go again;
My friend Glenn asks
"Jen, what did you do?"
"I don't remember," I say.

It's nice of Glenn.
He kindly says,
"Neither do I."

7-17-2000

I'm a Cat with Nine Lives

I saw a cat in the street.
I love cats so much.
I wish I could hold her in my arms.

Inexplicably,
I have a deep passion for cats.
I wonder
If in my previous life I was a cat.

People say,
Cats have nine lives.
I've gone through so much.
Maybe I was a cat.

I survived
A bad case of chicken pox.
I survived
A ski accident.
I survived
An electric car accident on a golf course.
Lately, I survived
An internal combat with depression.

Each time, seemed to my mom
A life-and-death tug-of-war.
Maybe I was a cat.
I have nine lives.

7-27-2000

We're Not Alone

I'm still awake;
Worried to death about my mama.
She is out at a meeting
Called the Parents of Children with Autism Support Group.

Seems like an eternity,
But she finally came home.
"Mom, what did you get out of the meeting?" I asked.

"Jen, we're not alone. I met Professor Peter Gerhardt
who will introduce us to more people
who may share similar problems."

We're not alone.
It sounds really fine.
For a very long time,
Mom and I have struggled along.

I can go to bed now.
My mama is home.
And it's good to know,
We're not alone.

7-21-2000

Not Worth a Scream

"My son doesn't complain
When he gets hurt and gets bruises."
It sounded familiar to Mom
When she listened to the statement
In the Parents of Children with
Autism Support Group last night.

It was exactly my case.
I always get bruises here and there
Without even knowing about them.

As for myself, I don't feel hurt that much;
Except when I see Mom's horrified eyes.
I don't know why.
I just don't feel the need to cry.

I'm not saying that I'm a person without pain.
It's just not worth a scream.

7-21-2000

Meeting with Dr. Gerhardt

I met Dr. Gerhardt with Mom.
He works for the Division of Adult and Transitional Service
On Douglas Campus of Rutgers University.

Upon entering the building I notice,
This is the place handling the autistic issues.
I am prepared.
For Mom has told me.

Autistic children do not speak well.
They cry and yell.
Crying and yelling is not my thing.
Not being able to speak well, indeed, is quite annoying.

I'm lucky.
Mom's been doing most of the talking and writing.
Together,
We discover many things piece by piece.
Writing poems brings us great joy and peace.

Dr. Gerhardt apparently is impressed by our working pieces.
He insists we try to get them published.
"Make sure to send me a copy with your autograph,"
He says sincerely.

Meeting with a professor like him,
Is truly encouraging.

8-02-2000

Adult Autism

Adult Autism is a strange term for me;
I need to adjust.

I'm so used to being alone,
Except with Mom and other family members.
Lately, I've been introduced into the Young Adult
Fellowship at church.

Adult Autism Support Group at Rutgers Campus
Is a new thing to me.
I have a hard time adapting to it.

I told Mom I wanted to go home.
She acknowledged it
And took me home.

I need more time
To adjust to the new environment
And the new group.
Mom was glad that
I told her how I felt.

Together we wish
The Adult Autism Support Group does well.
They are a nice group trying to cope.
Coping with living in society
As a big group.

8-07-2000

Perhaps

I went to see Dr. Shin.
He read through a small part of my poems,
It would be too many
If I showed him all of my poems.

I told Dr. Shin.
Someday,
I want to publish a poetry book.
He reminded me the publisher
Would want to make sure
My book sells off shelves.

Perhaps,
Publishers are profit-minded.
Perhaps, but
That is not a major concern.
Perhaps,
Angels will help.
And perhaps,
The book will reach out
To many people who need help.

7-24-2000

Sneaky Me

Sneaky me,
Eating the chicken meat.
Deep-fried with glazed honey from a bee.
Sorry Mama, my hungry stomach doesn't mean to be.
When I'm too hungry, the kitchen is the best place to be.
Excuse me, what else to eat?

6-28-2000

Jennifer is on medication. Her doctor has warned that the medication will give her side effects, including an increase in appetite. Her mom is watching over her diet.

Watch My Weight

Dr. Shin wants me to stay thin.
Dealing with weight issues, I've never foreseen.
Being skinny all my life I have been,
Until I got sick and was put on medication.

Paxil and Zyprexa I'm taking.
They help me calm down,
But also slow me down.
I have reduced the speed when I walk
Due to the medicine I'm taking.
Another side effect,
The medication makes me want to eat.
It is hard to fight the cravings.

Dealing with weight issues, I've never foreseen.
I used to be toothpick thin.
To gain more weight once was a dream.
But I never dreamed of getting it this way.
In six months,
I've gained more than ten pounds.

Holiday seasons are here.
Cookies, cakes, pies, and turkeys
Pass round and round.
But wait,
I have to
Watch my weight.

12-15-2000

Looking at the Light

I don't like it when people stare at me.
Mom said, "People like to look at the light."
She means that
If I have Jesus' light in me,
People want to look, not at me, but at the light.

Perhaps she is right.
I should share the light,
Instead of running away
From people's sight.

6-13-2000

I'm no Longer Afraid

I'm no longer afraid
When people are around.
I used to be
Especially, when I was not feeling well.
I thought
People were there to hurt me.

I prayed to God for His help and protection.
He listened.
He's set me free.
I'm no longer frightened.
I'm free to go places like
Supermarkets, shops and restaurants.

It's wonderful to be free.
I'm no longer afraid.

6-11-2000

Mom is Thinking about Dropping Courses

Mom called the college;
She is thinking about dropping courses.
It's been both a joy and a torture to take classes.
I enjoy going to school.
Sitting there and watching people is cool.
But when assignments and exams hit,
I can feel the volcano heat.

Many hours of memorizing and laboring,
My dear Mom's patience becomes dangling.
My brain is not functioning.
It picks up nothing.

My mom never loses her temper with me,
Only when the heat gets too much.
After studying a hundred times
I still have a hard time,
She gradually fall apart and break down.

I don't want to see my mom get frustrated
And breakdown.
I try and try and cry.
Thanks God.
It's been tough,
But we are all right.
Maybe all we need
Is to slow down.

7-10-2000

Break Free

As Mom and I walked along
The streets of Freehold,
We came upon a drug store at the street corner.
We decided to go in and
Get something to drink.

Inside the store,
A well-dressed old lady
Was chatting with the storeowner.
They were talking about political issues-
A recent accusation against our governor.

"I can't keep up with the news anymore.
I no longer read the daily paper," the old lady said.

"I don't either," I echoed.

The old lady turned and smiled at me,
"Let the world worry about you and me."

It might sound funny.
But whether you agree or not
News can drive people nuts.
I will abandon it for now
I need no more chaotic influences from the outside to
Upset me.
Break free.

7-14-2000

I'm a Unique Person not Like Anyone Else

My sister Jessie has been reading my poems.
She says that she understands me much better now.

It is nice to be understood,
I'm a unique person not like anyone else.

I appreciate people who accept me the way I am.
Being pushed to be someone else
Is nothing but heartbreaking.

I'm a unique person God has created.
I appreciate people leaving me alone
Until the day I come along.

7-17-2000

Priority Has Changed

Doreen, our dance teacher announced,
"If you're working on A's,
Please remember to choreograph your own dance."

Mom gave up;
This is not her style;
She used to be an "A" person;
But her priority has changed.

Ever since I got sick,
My health has become the top priority.
Nothing else can be above it,
Not grades, not speed, not perfection.

We are here to enjoy the class.
We are here to appreciate dance movements.
We are here also to enjoy our classmates.

Mom is happy to see me breathe.
She is ecstatic to see me smile.
She is fine to forget about getting A's.
Her priority has changed.

12-02-2000

Growing Pain

A Weird Dream

It was a weird dream:
I had seen another woman in my sleep.
Who was she?
And what was she doing in my dream?

I don't think I know her.
But strangely
I fell in love with her.

She was a blonde.
And she was young.
She gave me a gentle kiss on my lips;
I felt like a feather, being lifted.

It was a weird dream,
How strange.
I fell in love with another woman.

7-13-2000

If You Let Her Come In

I know a girl, who is lovable and sweet.
She will never break your heart.
Whenever you are not feeling well,
She will say a prayer for you.
Whenever you need a hug,
She will give it to you.

If you need a walk under the moonlight
She will be there by you.
She won't mind counting stars
Till dawn, till the day starts.

In spring,
She will gather flowers from fields
And bring them to your bedside.

In summer,
She will catch the ocean breeze and listen to seagulls
As ocean waves kiss you by your side.

Autumn arrives,
She will dance in the foliage
Collecting a whole basketful of color and fragrance.
You can then use a brush and paint it
Into your heart and mind.

In the deep winter night
She will listen to your stories by the fireplace
As crackling fire sings its melody.
Promise, she won't say good night.

I know a girl, who is lovely and sweet,
If you let her come in.

6-20-2000

What to Do? What Shall I Do?

Living in the next town to Colts Neck,
I get to visit the countryside often.
By its name
Colts Neck is a place with horses.

Horse farms dot here and there.
Handsome colts and their papa, mama folks
Graze around on the green pastures near farms.
They look graceful and relaxed.
In such a beautiful afternoon of *s*pring.

Under the clear blue sky I said to Mom,
"Being horses is not bad."
"Why?"
"They don't have to worry about work, but I do.
I don't know what to do and what shall I do?"

The next day I was sick
And was sent to the psychiatric ward.

If I were a horse,
I wouldn't have to worry so much about
What to do and what shall I do?

I'm not a horse,
Horse friends can't you tell me what to do?
What shall I do?

7-25-2000

Everybody is Working but Me

Everybody is working but me.
I've tried,
It is too hard for me.

Everybody is energetic but me.
I've tried,
It is still too hard for me.

What's wrong with me?
Maybe nothing is really wrong with me.
I'm just different and unique;
God is holding the future for me.

Everybody is working including me.
I've found
Volunteering is good for me.

Everybody is energetic including me.
I've found
Appreciating life is good for me.

7-4-2000

Simplicity

I know at my age of twenty something
      Supposedly,
          I should know a lot.

Knowing things like how to get a job
      A boy friend
      Become independent
      And deal with the IRS.

I should also know what is going on
      In the world
      In the nation
      In the region
      And in local towns.

I should not forget to catch up with
      The latest technology
      New movies
      Fashion
      And makeup.

This is an awful lot for me,
      Once
      All these things get into me,
      They get all churned up
      And cannot get out of me.

I know at my age of twenty something
      Supposedly,
          I should know a lot.

But at the mercy of my health condition,
    I can only go with simplicity.

7-31-2000

Inseparable

Mom and I are always together;
We are inseparable.
Some people may think we are unthinkable.
We go everywhere together.

Mom took me to the hospital, doctors,
And the speech therapist altogether.
When she couldn't come in the surgery or classrooms
She waited outside.
She cried when no one was in sight.

Mom picked me up at school many times
Whenever I missed the school bus home or
Didn't feel well at times;
She also spoke with my teachers
When I experienced a hard time.

Mom is there for me all the time.
The time when I fainted, choked or fell ill;
She's tried all her might to read my mind.

Now I've grown up and sensed
That people want to separate us.
"Being independent," is what
They say to wrap it up.

I was placed here by God.
It's God's gracious work, the
Mother-daughter relationship.
God's work should be honored.

Therefore,
Mom and I should stay together.
We are inseparable.

7-9-2000

Meow, Meow, Meow

You can call me Jennifer Meow;
"Meow, meow, meow," I say.

Since I was little,
I didn't speak the human language
That you said.
I only said,
"Meow…"

It was okay when I was younger.
It becomes strange,
If I'm still saying it.
I've stopped saying,
"Meow, meow, meow."

But I miss it a lot;
Growing up is no fun
Without meowing.

Don't ask me why.
I just love it,
"Meow, meow, meow."

7-17-2000

A Good-Looking Man

Jack is his name, a new karate classmate.
How come I've never seen him?

He is not a brand-new student,
I know it, because of his belt.
He is holding a high-ranking colored belt.

"Mom, look at that new guy. He's cute,"
I told Mom.
"Yes, he is quiet with a baby face."
Apparently, Mom also noticed him.

"Jen, do you have a crush on him?"
Mom joked
When I mentioned Jack the second time.

"No, I just appreciate good-looking men,"
I replied with a smile.

Right now,
I'd rather stay single.
Jumping into relationships with men
Is not yet my plan.

I appreciate good-looking men.
I don't mind being around them.

7-17-2000

It Has Been Coming Along

I used to think
I had trouble dealing with boys.
For I didn't have too many chances
being with them.

First,
I don't have brothers.
Second,
My father was not all that available.
Third,
My male relatives are difficult to reach.
They do not live in the same region.
Besides,
I'm a shy person
Who is never fond of social occasions.

Lately, God has helped.
He provides me nice brothers in Christ.
At first,
Mrs. Sun brought her son Michael to visit me.
Second,
Mrs. Shu also brought a son of hers, Peter,
And we hugged.
Third,
I've met many gentle and friendly brothers
Of the Young Adult Fellowship at church.

It has been coming along.
I feel a bit comfortable with boys now.

7-29-2000

A Hang-Out

So this is called a hangout.
I had never experienced one before.

Right now, I'm in a restaurant
Called "Applebee's",
With my church fellowship friends
Linda, Rob, Jason, Tim,
Anne, Daniel—and Mom.

Incredibly, I'm relaxed.
I used to think
Hanging out was beyond my reach.
I thought I would stress out.

My godly friends
Are extremely patient with me;
They don't rush or
Ridicule me.
Back in high school and junior high,
Kids there, used to.
They called names
And slung stones at me.

So this is called a hangout.
I'm in a restaurant with my friends
And Mom is included.
I'm going to tell Dad and Jessie
That I have a hangout.

8-04-2000
-Jessie is Jen's older sister.

I See, Then I See

I see Doreen, our dance teacher, with her husband and daughter.
I see Liz, one of our dance classmates, sitting alone in the audience.
I see Joan Cowell, our former family financial planner, and her
      boyfriend.
I see a young lady, who greeted me and said she was
In the master dance class with me once.
I see so many people at Pollack Theater at Monmouth University.
We are here to watch Ririe-Woodbury Dance Company's
Modern dance performance.
Then after the show, I see Jason, a member of my church's
Young Adult Fellowship,
Sitting alone at the bar at Applebee's.
Then I see Edward, another Young Adult Fellowship member
Walking in to meet Jason.
In one night, I see so many people.
It is incredible.
This has never happened before.
Before, I didn't go out at night.
I didn't hang out at places like the theater or Applebee's.
I feel good,
Although I'm hanging out with Mom instead of friends
Right now.

10-7-2000

I Won't Do It Again

I won't do it again.
Last night, I drove without a license
And without Mom sitting by my side.
Mom was in a meeting.
My license she was holding.
I didn't want to wait until the end of the meeting.
I drove the car away without permission.

I won't do it again.
It was scary to drive without Mom sitting by.
Beep-beep-beep
A car behind me wanted to pass by.
Beep-beep-beep
Another car honked.
I told myself, stay in control.
Even though it was scary, the car must proceed.

I won't do it again.
I saw Dad's expression
As I walked in the kitchen.
"Dad pick up Mom please," I said.
Dad dashed out the door with me following him.
There we went,
As fast as the wind.

I won't do it again.
When I entered the room,
Mom's friends burst out in cheers, the whole meeting room.
Mama wasn't there.
She was out with a friend to look for me everywhere.
Sorry Mama, I didn't mean to make you worry.

I'm glad the whole thing came to a happy ending.
I didn't get hurt.
Police didn't chase after.
Mama was a bit frightened,
But she managed to stay composed.
It was quite scary.
I promise,
I won't do it again.

6-30-2000

If I were a Twin

If I were a twin I could go to two places at the same time.
Or if I were part of a triplet, I could see even more.
Then I wouldn't have to choose between
Going to church, karate, or the beach.

If I were a twin I could stay in two places at the same time.
Or a triplet, I could stay even longer.
Then I wouldn't have to choose between
Staying in America, China, or Greece.

If I were a twin I could dream more.
Or a triplet, I could dream even wilder.
Then I wouldn't have to choose between
Becoming a wife, a nun, or a pilot.

6-28-2000

We Want, We Don't Want

This is not what I want.
The computer wouldn't stop running.
I pressed a wrong key,
The printer started to run and run.
A mile of paper flew out,
Like a flooded river.

Isn't this what we wanted?
Modern technology?
Automation and a magic wand?
But when things become not the way we want,
We just feel like we want to scream and run.

6-29-2000

Slow Down

Dear poems
Please slow down.
You've come about too fast,
Both Mom and I
Hate to let you pass.
But we're having a hard time
Jotting every thing down.

It's been fun.
But coming too fast
Can be exhausting
And tiresome.

Dear poems
Slow down
So we can do some other activities
Like walking around.

7-8-2000
-Dr. advised Jennifer to have daily walk.
It is important for her recovery.

We're on Our Own

Dear poems,
We're pretty much on our own.
My sister Jessie has been enjoying reading my poems,
But she is too busy to correct them.
Although my mom is willing to scratch her head and help out,
She complains that she is not a native English speaker.
I wish I could be my mom's help
But I have problems myself.

I have keen sense,
But I have a hard time getting it out.
I don't want to blame my sister.
She is a medical doctor,
And often she is busy,
And tired out.

So dear poems
We're pretty much on our own.
Please help me and help my mom out.

7-10-2000

I Wish He Was Single

Uncle Stanley said to Dad and Mom,
"Let's have some fun."
He took us to a dance club where older people
Wiggled under the instruction of a dance instructor.
The young instructor caught me on the floor,
For I'm the youngest dancer on the whole floor.

The instructor was handsome and nice.
He must be a male ballerina, or a knight.
With his graceful pose and exotic accent,
Someone told me he comes from a cold place
Where *Dr. Shivago* took place,
A place with many good dancers.

The instructor Gary invited me to dance
With him on the floor.
We looked into each other's eyes
And sailed before the eyes of hundreds of spectators.
I wish the instructor was single.
But what would it matter?
We would be going home soon, no matter.

12-17-2000
-Uncle Stanley is a family friend.

Cinderella with Wrong Shoes

This can't be happening.
I'm dancing with a prince from a foreign country.
Am I in a dream?

No, I am not in the dream.
I'm dancing with a good-looking young prince.
What is going on?
Am I a Cinderella in her prince's arms?

This just can't be happening.
Cinderella has her glittering shining shoes,
But I don't.
I'm wearing a pair of old street shoes.
No, it's not even street shoes.
It's a pair of old slippers.

I wish my prince didn't see my shoes.
I wish I was still sleeping,
So I wouldn't have to embarrass myself
With the wrong shoes.

12-17-2000

Nature and Animals

Holy Clouds

I see clouds
Day and night
They've been
Giving me
So much
Joy and peace
With their
Tranquility.

When I was little,
I used to see them
As lollipops,
As clowns.

Now that I've grown
I see them
As ocean waves,
As soft brushes
Painted by an awesome
God.

Oh, holy clouds
Take me into your house
I want to
Snuggle and
Shout.

7-6-2000

A Divine Secret

I bring winter wonders home
On a simmering summer's day.
A bag of winter-pine scent
Contains all its secrets.

I bring winter wonders home
On a simmering long summer day.
As I place the scent bag in each room,
The smell of cool winter pine
Starts to waft by.

It wafts through my mind and
Comes into my dream.
I see myself melt into
The summer forest
As winter pine, divine.

Rabbits come to find me
Robins rest on the branches of me
Squirrels play hide-and-seek
I hear the rambling brook pass by
I'm part of Nature
And Nature is a part of me.

A bag of winter pine scent
Contains all its secrets, divine.

7-11-2000

Sunbathing

I'm sunbathing in a foreign country
On a white sand beach.
I hear the ocean waves wash the seashells
With a soft whisper.

The sun is strong.
I have to put on my shades.
The tempo is slow.
I have to lay back
And enjoy a carefree
Summer day.

Dear Mama, don't drive too fast.
I don't want to get out.
I'm fine cruising inside your car.
With the seat down and
The air-conditioning on.

As you can see
I'm sunbathing in my Mama's car.
It's really a very cool thing to do.
Try it; you may like it as I do.

7-12-2000

The Life of Riverside

The new bridge between Red Bank and Middletown
has opened up this beautiful summertime.
I don't know the name of the bridge.
But I will call it Navesink Bridge
For it has spanned over the river
All this time.

The view
From the bridge in summertime is
Filled with sailboats, race boats, and jet skis.
If you stand on the bridge
Under a clear blue sky,
This picturesque scenery
Comes into sight.

There are classy mansions,
Dotting the woods along the riverside.
With those private docks and cabanas,
Who resides there?

Mom and I come to the riverside.
After meandering on the bridge a little while
We decide
To buy Italian ices at a little stand.

Mmmm…it's cantaloupe flavor, special.
Let's celebrate the life of the riverside.

7-1-2000

Thunder or Fireworks

Walking under the dark cloudy day,
I heard
Thunder rumbling in the distance.

"Looks like thunder is heading this way," Mom murmured.
"Mom, it's not thunder, it's fireworks," I said.

As our conversation continued
An airplane flew overhead
And a gush of water
Rushed through a pipe.

"Oh honey, maybe you are right.
Tomorrow is the Fourth of July all right."

But we still don't know what was exactly in the sky,
An airplane, fireworks or thunder…

Who was right? Mom or I?
Maybe both Mom and I.

7-3-2000

Fire Rain

Fire rain came pouring down
From the pitch, dark sky.
Cheers arose
As the rain lit up the sky.

Fire rain was coming down
From the beach sky.
Children sat
On their parents' laps
And looked up at the spectacular wonders
Above in that beautiful sky.

Fire rain was coming down
From the cloudless sky.
Suddenly, it turned into
Countless diamonds
Showering the sky.

Ocean waves were singing high
The Star Spangled onto the patriotic sky.
This is the firework celebration
For the Fourth of July.

7-4-2000
-on Point Pleasant Beach, NJ

The Plant is Gone

"The plant on the front porch is gone!"
Mom exclaims.

She is right.
The plant is gone.
Where could it be?

Well, the plant hasn't been doing well
Since its arrival at our home.
It was a gift from dad's patient.

The plant blossomed
With white flowers.
The flowers carried a special fragrance.
But now the flowers have withered
And the fragrance has gone.

Dad desperately
Wanted to give it to someone
With a green thumb.
I asked my friend Louisa who is a plant expert,
But she didn't want it.
She suggested rescuing it by putting it outside.
I did exactly what Louisa had said,
Put it out on the porch.

But now, the plant is gone.
Where could it be?

I bow my head.
Say a little prayer.
Whoever took the plant,
Please take good care of the poor plant.

7-9-2000

Please Open Up

Dear Lord,
Please open up the orchids
So that they can show their beauty
And be proud.

Dear Lord,
We've waited and waited
For the orchids to blossom.
It's been two years,
Since the last time we saw them.

Dear Lord,
Forgive us
Looks like we've watered them too much.
Right now the buds are nodding
And their heads seem heavy.

Dear Lord,
Please, please help
To open up the orchids.
Let their soft purple beauty return
And be proud.

7-9-2000

Everything is Beautiful

Sensei Hoffman
(the master of my karate school)
Called out for us to stop.
He wanted us to look out.
"What had happened?" I asked.
Everybody turned around and looked.
Wow, what a beautiful sunset.

Neon purple, pink, peach, and pastel blue…
Like an ocean of crystal wine had been brewed.
You want to drink it till you get drunk.
No need to do that, your heart has already drowned.
Drowned into that wondrous glory, one of many kinds.

I've been enjoying many sunsets of all kinds
Each time when I go out, walk about or drive around.
God is so wonderful.
He gives us all these wonderful nature wonders.

I want to shout out "thanks."
Thank you not only for the glorious wonders,
But for the wonderful people
Who embrace the sunrise, sunset and all the natural wonders.

Everything is beautiful.

7-10-2000

Rain

The clouds were so thick.
They were also dark.

All of a sudden, the sun was gone.
The bright summer disappeared.

Torrential rain started coming down,
Harshly and fiercely.

Until last night,
Harshness and fierceness ceased.
But the rain still came down.

I left the window open.
And listened to the sound.
It sounded like
A tropical rain forest.

I love rain.
It nourishes our land
And rinses all the dust away.

But after the rain,
I still look forward to
A bright sunny day.

7-15-2000

The Whole Town is So Quiet

Everybody is gone.
The whole town is so quiet.

There is a Christian crusade going on in New York City.
I know a lot of our church brothers and sisters are going,
But I don't get to go.
Mom worries that it will overwhelm me as well as her.
For thousands upon thousands of people will be there—
In Madison Square Garden.

The whole town is so quiet.
When I go out to walk
I feel that way too. Quiet.

But wait.
I see a few children
Playing on their front porches,
And a few bunnies are hopping.

The whole town is so quiet.
It seems to be at first.
But if I look further,
A few cars are passing by,
And the sun is peering out.

The whole town seems so quiet.
But yet,
It is not.

7-15-2000

Summer Outdoor Concert

The little puppy is so cute.
He wiggles himself in with his tailspins.
Little puppy, what are you doing?
The summer outdoor concert is performing,
Why do you look away not listening?

The little boys and girls are so lovely.
They run around and play.
Little boys and girls, what are you doing?
The summer outdoor concert is performing,
Why do you look away, and tumble about?

The sky above is soft and crystal blue.
This is a good place to take a little snooze.
The summer outdoor concert is performing.
The atmosphere is very relaxing.
Let me lie down and not worry about a thing.

7-20-2000

A Piece of Memory

It's been twenty years.
Twenty years ago I went through
Speech therapy with
A very nice lady, Mrs. Gaunt.

"Mom, can we find Mrs. Gaunt's house?"
As we drove through a waterfront town.

We found it.
It is in the heart of Fair Haven—
A quaint little town by Navesink River.

Things haven't changed much:
Nice country-style houses
With very well kept gardens.
Except the low, wooden white fences.
Those are new.

I enjoyed the white fences
Around each house in the neighborhood.
They add more country touches
With flower patches within.

Some sprinklers were turned on.
The whole neighborhood
Was quiet and calm.
I didn't see Mrs. Gaunt.
She probably wouldn't recognize me
If I knocked on her door,
And that's if she's still living behind that door.

It's nice to come back.
A nice little town,
A nice teacher,
A piece of memory.
And that quiet little Corner Café
Is still there where Mom used to wait.

7-23-2000

It is All Right

A white dog jumped out from the dark
When Mom and I went out for a walk last night.
His master called out, "Jesse, stop."
So his name is Jesse,
The white dog.

Maybe, to Jesse I'm a stranger;
But to me, he is not.
I've seen him many times on my walks with Mom.

Jesse barked at me.
Maybe he didn't recognize me.
His bark ruined my mood for watching night stars.
But it is all right.
He is just doing his job
To protect his master.

7-2-2000

A Romantic Thing

Ripples circle round and round on the pond
With charming grace and ease.
Ducks glide on.

Ducks my friends,
It's starting to rain now.
When rain gets heavy
Do you need a place to be?

Look at me.
My mom and I visit the park
With an umbrella close to our hearts.
You can share ours if you want.

Let me tell you a story, dear ducks.
My Chinese friend tells me a story.
She says that today is special;
It is the Chinese Valentine's Day.

A long, long time ago in China,
A young cowboy fell in love with a charming seamstress.
Their love was forbidden.
They were separated.
They were permitted to meet only once a year,
On the seventh day of the seventh lunar month, which is also today.

Perhaps, the raindrops are their joyful tears from the sky.
Dear friends, you glide.
Are you witnessing the great love of this kind?
I understand why you don't hide.

Although you get wet, you don't mind.
You are such a romantic thing.

8-06-2000 Holmdel Park in Holmdel, NJ
The seventh day of the seventh lunar
month usually falls in August
in the Gregorian calendar.

A Beautiful Afternoon

Serene and peaceful,
I savor this moment.
I'm at the Molly Pitcher Inn,
A historical site with classical touches within.
Mom and I enjoy our lunch in the dinning room
With a fabulous view of Navesink.
Blue skies carry
The reflections of the waterway to the ocean;
Puffy clouds smile and sing in delight.
A few tiny sparrows fly by,
And a few gulls too.

Sailboats one or two,
The rest are napping inside the marina.
This is a regular weekday noon;
Their owners probably have
Other things to do.

Serene and peaceful,
I savor this moment.
A beautiful afternoon,
I take it all in.

8-08-2000 Red Bank, New Jersey

Thanks for Keeping Up the Beautiful Backyards

Thanks for keeping up the beautiful backyards.
I see them from the waterway
Of Manasquan Canal from a boat.

I know
Before any backyard turns into an outdoor paradise,
It must start from scratch, piles of dirt, stacks of brick,
Huge labor and many devoted minds.

It's like
Composing a poem;
Many hours of thinking, dreaming and endless observation
Before it turns to a nice tune.

I'm looking at the beautiful backyards along the canal,
Realizing how much hard work
Has melted in.

Many thanks for keeping up the beautiful backyards.
Not only the poets enjoy their work,
As a passenger of a boat I share their joy.

7-7-2000

Guess Who Am I?

I'm on the water,
But I'm not a seagull.

I watch the elegant private yachts
Dock by the river;
But no way,
I'm not one of the yacht club members.

I embrace the sunset and golden clouds;
But you can't find me in the beach crowds.

Water waves gently wash in and out;
But wrong again, I'm not an ocean swimmer.

I feel the breeze
Drink the music
Dance bare-footed
Meet with a queen
And enjoy the most delicious cookies
Reserved only for a special young princess.

Guess who am I?

I'm a Jersey princess,
Indulging herself on the River Queen.
The boat goes around the
Manasquan inlet with the wind.

7-7-2000

A Dragonfly

I saw a dragonfly
As I stepped outside.

Dragonfly,
How come you don't fly?
Is it too hot outside?

I agree.
It is scorching hot.
I would stay motionless too.
When I come inside I find
A nice place to hide.

I saw a dragonfly,
As I stepped outside.
Its wings are fairylike.
Its body is like a sleek yacht.

Dragonfly,
How come you don't set foot in China?
Is it too far away to fly?

I understand.
It is across the ocean on the other side.
My dad said,
He once saw a dragonfly in China—
Must be your ancestor, dragonfly.

7-4-2000

A New Friend Visits Me

A new friend visited me today.
Guess who it was?

Let me give you a hint.
He lives in nature with wings.

Oh, he is also green and jumpy.
That's the second hint.

"Mom, don't touch him.
He is my friend,"
I said when I saw him.

I have no clue where he's from,
Or how he got in.
He just stands there
On the curtains in my room.

Can you guess who my visitor is now?
Come on
You can do it, if you try.
Time is ticking by.
Let me give you a hand and spell it out:

G-r-a-s-s-h-o-p-p-e-r

7-21-2000

A Dog and A Little Girl

She is running wild in the rain,
A dog with wet hair.

Mom and I were startled,
When we saw a bunny
Hop out from the woods.
The bunny looked unsettled.

Then running after the bunny
Was this mad dog,
A hefty one with large strides.

"Allie, Allie…" someone was calling.
So, the dog is not a stray; she has a master.

A father and a little girl appeared.
They were holding leashes in their hands.

"Don't worry. She is on a leash,
Whoever is out there in the street,"
The little girl called out to us
From the other side.

I heard the little girl say to the dog,
"Bad girl. You got yourself wet."
I'm glad that the father and the little girl
Found their dog.
They are now together.

7-30-2000

Stay Happily Ever After

I saw a deer family in the woods.
This was not my first time seeing deer.
But seeing a deer family
Was something else.

Last time,
I saw a white-tailed mama deer and her calf in our yard.
"Mom look, mama deer and her baby," I called out.
My mama wrote a Chinese poem
About what she saw.

This time I saw not only mama and the calf,
I saw the papa too.
It is my turn to write them into one of my poems.

I wish the deer family happy and healthy.
I know there is an issue about deer overpopulation
In New Jersey.

I just hope no one will hurt them.
They will stay happily ever after,
Safely wandering in nature.

8-01-2000

I Hope You Didn't Get Hurt

Poor rabbit,
I hope you didn't get hurt.

What was that squeaky noise
I just heard?
The woman in the driver's seat looked horrified.

Poor rabbit,
I hope you didn't get hurt
Or frightened.

Next time,
Be more careful
When you hop across the street.

Although this is the countryside,
It's the era of automobiles
And tractors, besides.

Poor rabbit,
You probably don't know
What these modern hazards are about.
But be very careful.
I don't want you to get hurt.

8-01-2000

Wishes For Kittens

Two little kittens, about a week old,
They were so tiny, a little palm could hold them.

They were snuggled up inside a cardboard box.
The man said he found them.
The little kittens had been abandoned.

Poor little things,
Do not cry.
Everything is going to be all right.
You are going to stay here at the shelter
Only for a little while.
We will find you a right home in no time.

Look now,
One of the little kittens
Climbed out.

Little Kitten,
Don't go out.
Is it your mama that
You are looking for?

I cupped the little one.
Gently put it back into the box
With the other one.
I then caressed them
One by one.

Little kittens,
Do not cry.
We will find you
The best home
As fast as we can find.

11-27-2000
-Jen volunteers at SPCA animal shelter.

Crows Everywhere

Crows everywhere—
Some are on our lawn,
Some on our neighbors'.

When I walk outside
I see crows fly by;
They don't fly high,
Nor do they sing right.

Crows everywhere—
When I visited Lisa's house
They were there.
One bad crow swooped down
And snatched a baby bunny
Away from Lisa's backyard.
Poor little Danica started to cry.

Crows everywhere—
The next-door neighbor Mr. Wang once told Dad,
Whenever he saw crows,
He didn't feel well.
The black birds brought bad luck, he said.

I asked Mrs. McNally, my pastor's wife,
How good can crows be?
She pondered a little and answered me,
"Eating garbage is one of the things they do."

I don't care what they do.
Seeing them everywhere

Isn't the most pleasant thing,
As far as I'm concerned.

6-29-2000
-Lisa is the Youth Director
at Monmouth Chinese
Christian Church
In New Jersey.
Danica is Lisa's
two-year-old daughter.

The Fish

Holding its breath,
A commotion is going on.
A fish, grass carp, I guess,
Is flipping around in a fish tank.
What is going on?
Why is he so hyper?

Now the tank is filling with water bubbles.
I don't see any other fish;
Only the grass carp splashes and swishes.
He twitches his body like crazy.

Looks like he is really scared and frightened.
Is he screaming about something?
He may be gasping,
"Help, help, help."
Or may be pleading,
"Go away, leave me alone."

It is too late—oh too late,
A net is coming.
The grass carp is still struggling.
He struggles in vain.
Now he is trapped in the net.

I'm sorry I can't help.
I'm sitting in a restaurant with a fish tank.
In a few minutes the fish will become a gourmet dish.

Then it will sit in someone's stomach.
I hope it won't end up on my table.
I'm not sure my stomach can handle it.

12-28-2000

Family

Last Me the Whole Life Long

Grandfather has been sick;
He has cancer.

I've been praying for him fervently;
But in reality,
One day he may leave us.

It's ironic.
Grandfather used to be vigorous and stern
But now he lies there
Lifeless.

I've always lacked what grandpa had.
But strangely
He never got upset with me.
He used to be angry
With anyone who was sheepish.

Mom once told Grandpa,
"Dad, Jen has problems.
She won't be able to achieve
What you want."

Grandpa was silent, for a few seconds.
Then very gently
He nodded his head.
Miraculously,
Grandpa spared me.

Not long ago,
Just before he slipped into unconsciousness

He told Mom,
"Please take care of Jen."

Grandpa and I never spent much of our time together;
But he loves me in a special way.
That alone
Lasts me the whole life long.

8-3-2000

Grandpa, Have a Nice Trip

Mom's sister Regina called from Taiwan;
Grandpa isn't doing well;
His health condition is taking a sharp turn.

Two nights ago I woke up
In a dream and told Mom
I wanted to go back to see Grandpa.

The next day I forgot what I had said.
When Aunt Regina called and told
What had happened with Grandpa
Exactly two days ago,
Mom received it with grace.
She didn't lose her hold.

I pray that God receives Grandpa
With extra kindness and holiness;
Grandpa is not yet a Christian
But I hope his soul can be saved.

Mom told me,
Grandpa is ready to be with his parents.
We should bless him and peacefully
Send him off to heaven.

I agree with Mom:
No more tears and struggles.
I'm ready to let go.
Grandpa, please have a nice trip home.
I love you.

8-04-2000

With God, Nothing is Too Hard

Mom is calling her older brother, Uncle Jerome, on the phone,
Telling him that Grandpa's condition
Is in a downward spiral.

Uncle Jerome used to have many issues with Grandpa,
Same as my mom.

I heard that Grandpa was pretty tyrannical
With his own children;
But he never treated his grandchildren
That way.

I love Grandpa,
Although he made mistakes in the past.
I wish Uncle Jerome and my mom can make peace
With Grandpa and their past.

It may be hard;
But with God
Nothing is too hard.

8-04-2000

Sing

Here is the intensive care unit at the hospital.
Both Grandma and I
Stand by Grandpa's bedside.

Grandpa is very ill, very skinny and dry.
Dehydration makes his bones have nowhere to hide.
He has shrunk and looks strange.
I barely recognize him.
Grandpa does not move,
He lies still, very still.
I wonder if he knows that I've traveled from America
And love him very much still.

Poor Grandpa,
He is all hooked up with IV tubes.
I start the musical tunes
"Jesus Loves You," and "Amazing Grace"
As loud as I can sing.

Grandpa still doesn't move.
I don't care.
At this moment, this is the only way
to communicate.

I see Grandma's eyes smile with tears.
I wish Grandpa could hear and feel.
Hear my songs and feel Grandma's tears.
Maybe, through the divine he will.

Grandpa,
I hope angels come and help you through.
I will keep singing until it becomes true.

8-14-2000

Grandpa Squeezed Me

"Mom, I feel a squeeze from Grandpa,"
I told Mom as I stepped out of the ICU.

It has been a couple of days
Since I've started singing for Grandpa.
I feel his squeeze very gently, very slightly
While I sing and hold his hand.

Grandpa can't talk
But he is listening.
I know it.
I sense it.

"Mom, Grandpa squeezed me,"
I said with excitement.

Angels must be around.
Grandpa is responding.
Oh, thank you angels
You are wonderful.

Grandpa,
You're going to be alright.
I know it.

8-17-2000

He is My Father

Grandpa is out of the ICU.
I knew he would become better.

He is still weak,
Very, very weak.

His sons and daughters
Are around to comfort him.

Memories bring me back,
Back to the first day we arrived.
Dad, Mom, and I
Rushed to the hospital
Straight from the airport.

Mom pushed the ICU door open.
The room was quiet and open.
A white-uniformed doctor with his back to us
Was writing.

Mom looked down at the nametags.
She found her father.
The man lying on the bed looked like a skeleton.
Could he be Grandfather?

A nurse in the room sensed our presence.
She turned around with an angry look.
"It's not visiting hours," she protested.
"He is my father. I'm his daughter from America,"
Mom pleaded.
The nurse didn't listen.
She chased us out in an instant.

That was about ten days ago.
I'm glad Grandpa is out of the ICU.
His children no longer need
Permission to go in and see him now.

8-21-2000

A Strong Lady

Grandma is always giving.
She brings gifts to us
When she visits America.

Grandma never stops giving.
When we visit her in Taiwan,
She brings me to shops.
"This would look good on you.
Try it, Jen."
As a result,
I get a lot of goodies:
Shirts, pants and shoes.

Grandma walks very fast.
For her age of seventy four
She walks faster than young folks do.
She walks faster than any of her children.
When we walk with her,
Mom, Aunt Regina and I often end up
Falling behind.

Sometimes Grandma suddenly remembers
We are following.
She stops, turns and looks at us
With that lovely smile of hers.

Grandma always smiles.
She has a spirit filled with
Gentleness, kindness and happiness.
Although, Grandpa is sick at the hospital,
Grandma never forgets to bring her smile.

Grandma is petite—only about five-foot tall.
She keeps herself fit and stands up tall.
I admire a strong lady like her.

8-22-2000

The Way

God has been teaching
Dad and Mom
How to glide.

Dad and Mom
Used to be shaken up
Whenever they stood face to face
In crises.

In April earlier this year,
I got sick—really, really sick.
Mom almost lost her faith.
Dad prayed; Mom cried.
Then both of them
Prayed and cried.

They cried out to God
To help me and set me free.
God listened.
He made me recover
And the stormy weather passed.

Dad and Mom
No longer sob
When storms,
And tidal waves
Come their way.
They simply pray.

God has taught them
The way.

7-27-2000

Swing Straight, Swing Out

Swing straight.
Swing Out.
The balls fly far away out.

Arms straight.
Back straight.
They are not supposed to sway.

Here is the Fairway golf range in town.
I don't come here all the time.
Today I'm here with Dad
Because we have to kill time.

Mom is spending her special time
In a salon around town.
Dad and I might as well have a good time.

Swing straight.
Swing out.
The balls fly far away out.

Not only Dad and I are having fun.
I see fathers, mothers, grandpas, grandmas,
And children also having a day of fun.

Look at the far end corner, a pair of lovers is playing out.
They get their energy worked out;
The love relationship also flows out.

Swing straight.
Swing out.
I thank Dad for taking me out.

7-6-2000

Funny Mom

My Mom can be funny sometimes.
In what way? you may say.

Here is one example.
Last night I took a walk with her.
Mom asked,
"Jen, are you in one piece?"

I burst into laughter and replied,
"Yes Mom I'm in one piece.
Or are you talking about a bathing suit?"
Of course, my mom wasn't talking about a bathing suit.
She just wanted to make sure I was intact
In the darkness.

My mom can be really funny sometimes.
One day,
She saw a car passing by.
"Look, a topless car,"
She cracked into a good laugh
Right after she said that.

What can I do with my Mom?
She pronounces my church friend Ed's name
As "Egg."

My Mom wasn't born in America;
She can be so funny sometimes,
But let her be, never mind.

7-19-2000

Must Be the Wind

"Must be the wind," Mom sings it out as a tune.
I smile and echo her.
Then we laugh at each other.

Mom thinks it is very cute
When I tell her this American expression.
I tell her,
Whenever she hears something like w h o o s h going on,
She must say, "must be the wind."
Mom has no problem with it.
She repeats and carries it out as a tune.

I ask Mom,
What do Chinese people do
When someone accidentally passes gas?
Mom says,
"S-h-h-h…"
You are supposed to be quiet and wish the embarrassing situation
Will quickly pass through.

Different cultures react differently to one situation.
Mom loves particularly this American expression.
"Must be the wind," she sings.
She thinks it is the cutest thing.

6-30-2000

You Are Cold

Here we go again.
Mom said to our karate class friend Loli,
"You're cold."
I looked at Mom and smiled at her when I overheard it.

Mom was pairing up with Loli who was tough but nice
With a wonderfully warm heart.
Although Loli has a very warm heart, her hands are cold.
That was exactly what Mom was telling her,
"Loli, you're cold."

Loli puzzled a second and said to Mom,
"Oh, my hands are always cold."

I was glad that Loli picked it up and let Mom go.

7-31-2000

I Love My Sister

I admire Jessie, my only sister.
She is five years older.
I used to go in her room,
When she was out.

I was curious to find out
What made my sister
Stand out.

She was in the gifted program,
And her many talents
Won her trophies in various contests.
Jessie excelled in roller-skating,
Dancing, cheerleading and
Science competitions.

And the most unique achievement of all:
Jessie won the title of
Miss New Jersey National Teenager in 1988.
I got to go to Hawaii with her.
Of course,
I am very proud of my sister.

I have stopped going into her room.
She is not there anymore.
She is now a medical doctor
Who has time no more.

I know she is a wonderful,
Remarkable doctor.
But I love her, not for
All her achievements,

But for the fact that
She is my sister.

7-28-2000

A Belated Birthday Gift

A gift
Comes from my sister.
It is late,
But it is fascinating.

The gift is very special,
It is a free Swedish massage
At Osaka Traditional Spas
In New York City.
Jessie and Mom accompanied me.
They waited outside while I was receiving my massage.

It hurt at first,
Then the pain softened.
A well-trained Hispanic woman
Worked on my body.
I was nude,
Covered only by a towel.

Staying in a semi-lit room for an hour,
Where the woman banged, pinched,
And rubbed me from head to toe.
Each piece of my muscles screamed,
But were nicely cleansed.
And I survived.

The gift was belated,
But certainly appreciated.

10-22-2000
-Jen's birthday was in April.
She was in the hospital at that time.

Slow Down Sister, I Can't Keep up

Dear sister,
Please slow down.
My feet hurt.
And my heart is racing.

I know you have a good heart.
You've taken me to a spa.
And you've just taken Mom and I to see Queen Latifah.

I appreciate what you have done for me,
But after the show, can you slow down your steps?
I just can't keep up.

New York City streets are hectic.
The temperature is extremely cold.
I can't move fast.
I am bundled up.
And my feet hurt.

Besides, Mom also had a hard time
Catching up.
Look at her,
It is like someone has just tossed dirt across her face.
I appreciate what you have done for me.
But slow down
Before my lungs fall out.

12-13-2000

A Star or a Doll

Cousin Hanping sent me an email.
She had just attended a women's safety awareness seminar
And wanted to share it with the people she loves.
I'm glad that
She included me.

Hanping loves me.
When I was in the hospital
She came with
Flowers, cards, pastels and drawing pads.
And of course with lots of love and her sweet hugs.

I love Cousin Hanping very much.
She is petite, delicate and very special.
She reminds me of a china doll.

She wears a short hairstyle
That matches perfectly with her smile.
One day,
My sister Jessie persuaded her
To cut her hair to super short.
The china doll became a bald doll.

With the shining bald head
Cousin Hanping shone.
She now shone like a singer or a movie star.
Hanping had a hard time with her mom.
She wanted Cousin Hanpin to grow her hair back
As long as a doll's.

I don't care what her mom said,
I love Cousin Hanping
The way she was
And the way she is now.
It doesn't matter to me
Whether she is a movie star or a china doll.

6-29-2000

Friends

A Long Time Ago

Recently, I saw Joan Cowell again.
She is a financial broker
Who worked with my parents
A long time ago.

"Hi, Jen, long time no see," she happily called out.

"Mom, Joan didn't do a good job, did she?"
I asked my mother later on.
"No honey, unfortunately.
But that was a long time ago."

I guess Joan was forgiven.

"Jen, I've also suffered from depression," Joan said
When she learned that I was recovering after a bad experience,
She shared hers with me.
"Besides my depression, I also lost my fiancé," she said.

"I'm sorry, Joan. When did this all happen?" Mom spontaneously asked.
"Not long ago. He died in a car crash."
"I'm so very sorry," we said.
Both Mom and I felt her pain.

I hope,
Someday Joan's pain will pass by.
When things fade away into a long time ago,
They don't hurt as much.

I really hope
A long time ago will do its trick.

She is Not My Mom

Mrs. Kuo came over.
Her daughter Josephine is getting married.
Mrs. Kuo said she didn't have time
To shop for herself.
"I'm not the fashion type,
And I'm shy," she said.

She came to borrow
Something to wear to the wedding
from Mom.

She tried on
The long, ivory satin gown.
What a beautiful woman Mrs. Kuo had become.
She'd turned into a charming swan.

Mrs. Kuo turned and turned and smiled.
"I never knew I had so much charm,"
She said it as I admired.

But wait,
Her son Eric had a strange look on his face.
"What's wrong," Mom asked.
"She is not my mom," Eric answered solemnly.

I said to myself.
Can't his mom be beautiful at least once?
I guess not,
Eric wants his mom.

A Heavenly Thing

To be able to enjoy and hug one another
Is a heavenly thing.
I found it in the Young Adult Fellowship at church,
Especially when we sing.
We sing to the Lord Jesus that
We are His special, special thing.
He died on the cross to cleanse our sins.
Do not worry about a thing.
Our faithful Lord will take care of everything.
Being at YAF in God's house
Is a wonderful thing.

*Young Adult Fellowship of
Monmouth Chinese
Christian Church has been
wonderful for Jen.
6-29-2000*

God's Love Flourishes

Sara, my fellowship friend,
Has been suffering epilepsy for years;
Poor Sara she has to live with it
All this time.

I pray that some day
Medical researches will find
A way to cure it, and that
Sara will be set free.

Sara shook uncontrollably today
At the fellowship meeting;
She was having another seizure attack.

I wish I knew how to help;
Luckily our fellowship leader Linda
And Sara's husband James
Came quickly to her aid;
Linda patted her back,
While James supported her
From falling.

Although,
I felt a sense of helplessness,
I witnessed love.
Love from God at this critical moment
Through the acts of Sara's loving husband
And her friend Linda.

Maybe there are questions of
Why illness, some of us have to bear.

Since God allows it to happen,
There must be something to learn.

Do not worry.
God will help.
Through our ups and downs during our lifetimes,
Friends, families bind together.
While we are experiencing inevitable hardships,
God's love flourishes.

8-04-2000

He Will Lead Us to His Door

Lisa called.
She was back from the short-term mission trip to Chicago.

Lisa had helped me a lot.
In addition of helping other youngsters at our church,
She spent time with me.

Ever since I was discharged from the hospital,
Lisa had opened her home to me.
She welcomed Mom and me to study the Bible with her.

Lisa told us
Her mom died when she was a teenager.
She turned her loneliness and fear
All onto the gracious King.

Lisa has God with her.
She has been doing great jobs for the Lord.
I'm amazed how God's wonderful power
Has poured onto her.

Lisa encourages Mom and me to hand over our difficulties
To the Lord;
The faithful God will never disappoint us.
He will lead us to his door.

7-27-2000
Lisa is the youth director of
Monmouth Chinese Christian
Church in New Jersey.

Danica Isn't Feeling Well

Danica isn't feeling well;
She has a sore tongue.
When she puts a piece of watermelon in her mouth,
It hurts her tongue and she starts to cry.

Although Danica cries and whines
She still plays with her toys.
As Danica plays,
She forgets all about the discomfort in her tongue.

Danica is a wonderful child.
Danica is an innocent girl.
When she hurts, she cries.
When she plays, she smiles.

I pray that she gets better very soon,
So she can be as happy as a kite
Fly high into the sky.

6-30-2000
-Danica is Lisa's two-year-old
daughter.

Passionate Friendship

They may look old,
But they are young at heart.
They certainly know how to hug.

When I don't feel well,
I go to them.
They extend their warm friendship
With plenty of food and passion.

I don't have to pretend,
I love their food;
I also love their passionate friendship

5-30-2000
-Pine Fellowship of Monmouth
Chinese Christian Church gave Jen
Great support during her recovery.

Barbara Livingston

Barbara Livingston was a missionary.
When you saw her,
You could sense in her the divine.
She had spent 45 years of her life
In Taiwan where my parents are from.

Barbara spoke no Chinese
When she first arrived in Taiwan;
But she managed to learn it well
Over the years.

Barbara came to Young Adult Fellowship to share her experience
today.
She said
The Chinese language she learned from books didn't help her at first,
For many, many dialects were spoken in Taiwan.

Through her faith,
She overcame the difficulty of language barriers.
Besides, she overcame the cultural shock and
The distinctiveness of her Caucasian look.

Looking back, she was grateful.
She thanked God for giving her the opportunity to experience
Taiwan.
Throughout the years she made many Chinese friends young and old.

Although Barbara is older now and retired,
She still came to our church.
She visited me when I was in the hospital.

She prayed with me during my difficult recovering period;
She also routinely wrote me cards to cheer my spirit.
God bless her—a wonderful daughter of the holy Father.

8-14-2000

A Surprise Gift

I'm looking at the color chart,
Hoping I can describe the colors
Which I see in the garden of
Dearborn Farm in our town.

I give up.
No matter how hard I try,
I know it will still fall short
From what I really want to describe.

In the garden of Dearborn Farm,
I see
A lily pond with a frog statue,
And a stream of spring water flows out from the frog's mouth.
Wind chimes ring about in the air like heavenly sounds.

Mom and I came to pick up a flowerpot
With an Oriental design all around it.
We want to give it to Pastor and his wife, Mrs. McNally
As a gift for a nice surprise.

The McNallys will return home
From a mission trip tomorrow.
Before they left for the trip,
They had helped me a lot,
Especially during the time I was in and out of the hospital.
I thank God for them and I miss them a lot.

Mom and I leave the flowerpot at their door- steps.
When leaving we take a second look at the flowerpot,

Both Mom and I like it a lot.
I hope the McNallys will like it too.

7-13-2000

Louisa

Louisa is a lady whose husband is a member of our church.
Although she is not yet a Christian,
She is truly a nice person with a big heart.

As she joined Joy Fellowship with her husband Bill,
I also joined the same group with my parents.
Joy Fellowship is a Christian group consisting of
A nice bunch of empty nesters.

It was so nice of the group that they not only welcomed Louisa,
They welcomed me too.
Louisa and I became good friends through the fellowship.
I enjoyed her gourmet cooking as well as her laughter.
She visited me with her delicious food as I came home from the
    hospital;
She also made me purple bracelets as special gifts.

I felt sorry that when she invited me to play golf with her,
I disappointed her by not being able to get up early enough
Due to the medicine I took.
Louisa grumbled about my sleepy head in her special friendly laughter;
I knew although Louisa was disappointed, she still loved me the
    same way.

7-24-2000

She is a Dance Teacher, Not a Science Teacher

Dr. Vera Chen is a science teacher
At Holmdel High School where I used to attend.

I've never been in her class,
For I studied outside mainstream classes.
Resource room was where I stayed
Along with other learning disabled students.

Although, I wasn't in her class, I knew her;
She was a good teacher.

I'm so glad that I got to be much closer with her
After I got out of high school and met her
At Joy Fellowship group
Where Dr. Chen and my parents belong.

I also had a chance to go on a local cruise ride with her.
Dr. Chen and I enjoyed a beautiful sunset on the ship deck together.
As the stars came up and the moonlight shone,
She held my hand and invited me to dance with her.
We danced round and round on the floor until the party's end.

To me, since that night,
I now consider
Dr. Chen a good dance teacher of mine;
I totally forgot about her as a science teacher.

7-10-2000

Mother and Son

Mrs. Sun is Mom's friend, also one of our church members.
Mrs. Sun's first son, Michael, is about my age.
Both the mother and the son are very nice.

When I was sick, Mrs. Sun brought Michael to visit me.
She brought me a poetry book to read.
She also brought me a pot of homemade chicken soup.
Mrs. Sun and Michael came to study Bible and sang songs with me.
Very kindly,
Mrs. Sun also walked around the neighborhood with me.

I heard she is going to relocate to China with her husband.
I'm going to miss her and Michael so much.
What a wonderful mother and son;
I pray that they will forever stay in the godly sun.

7-14-2000

For the Unselfish Reason We Let Go

I know I'm not the only one who loves Mrs. Sun;
God loves her,
Her husband and sons love her,
So do her friends and colleagues,
Especially her godly friends
From Joy Fellowship.

We will miss so much of her singing, storytelling,
And sweet praying; and
What about her brilliant smiles?
And her sunshine-like kindness?

God wants his children to go and bear fruit,
Mrs. Sun and her husband Mr. Sun
Certainly will serve to please God;
For they have that special gift and talent
From the highest above—our heavenly Father.
For that, we thank the Lord!

Our loss is others' gain;
For the unselfish reason,
We let go.

Our dear brother and sister
John and Daphne Sun;
May God be with you all the way
And all the day.

We will miss you night and day;
Maybe we will all visit you
Someday.

For the unselfish reason,
We let go;
May God bless you thousand-fold,
Much more than gold.

8-04-2000
-Mr. and Mrs.
Sun are relocating to Beijing China

A Special Friend

Christmas cards fly in.
It's the season for greeting.
One card stands out.
Oregon is the place it's from.

A photo of a young man whom I've never met.
His name is Roger and
He's enclosed a book of Oregon Coast cards
Plus a message for me.

Roger says,
"Thank you so much for thinking of me
And praying for me.
We've never even met.
Yet you thought of me in my difficult days.
I consider you a truly good friend."

Roger's father came to our house two years ago
With a bad news of Roger being in the hospital.
His son Roger was involved in a car accident.
He was in a deep coma.
While Dad looked at Rogers' brain scan
The father had brought,
Mom and I prayed with Roger's dad.

The prayer worked.
Roger awoke.
Two years have passed.
Roger has relearned how to walk, speak,
And work with his computer.

I'm so glad for Roger.
It's a miracle God has offered.
I'm graciously honored
To be a special friend of Roger's.

12-25-2000
-Jen's dad is a neurologist

Mr. Wu's Hope and Joy

Mr. Wu was a successful businessman,
Swift, smart and strong.
Mr. Wu decided to move to Gleneden Beach, Oregon
A couple of years ago, after he'd made a fortune.
He felt he had reached to the top and was ready to retire.

Then Mr. Wu almost was swallowed
By a tumultuous wave as he walked his dog
Along the beautiful beach of Oregon coast.
Six months later his son Roger was in a coma
By a car accident.
Mr. Wu was humbled.
He no longer felt he was sitting on top of the world.

Mr. Wu held back his tears while praying with Mom and I.
Mom told him Roger was an angel.
Roger would bless the family with the ordeal,
As Jen has blessed ours, she said.

Roger indeed is an angel.
Not only has he recovered from a bad car accident,
But with great spirit.
He brings his family joys.

This is what Mr. Wu's Christmas card
To my parents said:
"We always think of you with gratitude.
And every day we're comforted by your words:
'People like Jennifer and Roger are angels.'
You're so right and so wise."

I don't know if Roger and I are true angels.
But if so, I don't mind.

12-25-2000

A Girl As Quiet As Me

I met a girl, her name is Yi-Hua.
She is Cousin Hanping's cousin—
A quiet girl, like me.

She is pure and simple like a lily;
Lovely and sweet as a bunny.
The best of all,
We're about the same age.

Cousin Hanping brought her over to my house.
We enjoyed a good time with one another.
An afternoon of playing golf and
Walking around the seaside neighborhood,
Nothing was fancy but relaxing.

I am glad to meet a girl as quiet as me.

5-30-2000

I Look and Look

I look and look
A young Greek girl
Holding two pigeons stands before me.
It is a postcard from a new friend Yi-Hua I just met.

I look and look
The card is from the Metropolitan Museum of Art
Where my new friend must have visited.
For on the upper left corner of the card,
It says the Metropolitan Museum of Art.

I look and look
I see my friend browse around the museum.
She must have appreciated
All the artwork in each room.

I look and look
I see myself there too.
Oh, it must have been years
Since the last time I visited the grandeur of those rooms.

I look and look
A thank you note I took from my drawer.
I'm going to write to my new friend
What a nice thing for her to send me the card.

6-10-2000

My Friend Went to France

My Friend Yi-Hua sent me another postcard
With a photo of the *Louvre*.

In case someone doesn't know what the *Louvre* is,
It is the museum housing Mona Lisa and Venus de Milo
And many other great artwork of the world.

I bet you don't want to miss visiting the *Louvre*
When you go to France.
I know I won't.

I was going to go to France like my friend Yi-Hua did.
But I got sick right before the trip, unfortunately.

Well, I can go next time.
Enjoying it from the postcard is still fine.

7-8-2000

Chinese Calligraphy

Chinese calligraphy—it looks easy,
But doing it is not.
Mom's friend Mr. Chang volunteers to show me.

First, I have to learn a bit of history about this Chinese calligraphy:
There are seven styles of Chinese characters, developed through
The evolution of Chinese writing.
It must have been thousand of years since the first ancient words
were formed.

Next, to do Chinese calligraphy,
I have to sit up right
And hold the brush tight
Mr. Chang makes me trace on a special paper
Which is made out of rice.

He tells me,
Go up and go down and pause.

Go left and go right and pause.

Although I have a little trouble doing it,
I'm proud of myself.
It's not as easy as I thought it would be.
Yet Mr. Chang encourages me,
He says, if I keep on practicing,
I will someday surprise myself.

7-8-2000

Kevin, the Next-Door Neighbor's Boy

Kevin, the next door neighbor's
Little boy came over.

He came over with his dad and mom,
Mr. and Mrs. Wong.
Mr. and Mrs. Wong planned
To remodel their bathrooms.
The whole family came over to
Take a look at ours.

While Mom showed Mr. and Mrs. Wong up and down,
I kept Kevin company and played around.

Kevin said, "Hey, you have a nice place."
And I said, "Thank you."

Kevin is only four years old.
But he certainly is sociable
And very adorable.

7-19-2000

Travel

Holy Spirit Helps Me

Holy Spirit helps me pack.
I'm going away
To a far, far place.

My grandpa is very sick.
Mom, Dad, and I
Are going together.

I know I want to pack
Something simple.
I don't know about
My mom.
I hope she gets everything
Under control.

Holy Spirit, help not only me.
My mom, dad, grandpa and
Other family members need
You too.
Please bring us peace,
Happiness, and health.

Holy Spirit please help me.
Watch over
My sister Jessie,
Cousin Han-Ping
And my church friends
Who are not going
On this trip.

Holy Spirit, I thank you.
I know You are

More than willing to,
If we let you.

8-10-2000

Night Sky

It is one past midnight.
Our airplane is still waiting to
Be taken to the sky.

The plane is supposed to be leaving at twelve
From New Jersey for Taiwan.
One hour has passed, the plane is still not moving.

"We will be on our way,"
The captain keeps on repeating.
But the plane is still sitting.

It is hard to imagine.
The night sky is still busy.
I thought the sky at night should be quiet,
Joined only by stars, clouds, and moonlight.
Maybe with a few airplanes flying by.
Apparently, I was wrong.
It isn't so.

Poor sky,
Your life isn't as good as mine.
I get to enjoy quietness in my life.
If I wasn't traveling afar to see my grandpa,
I would probably be tucked away in bed at this hour.

Poor sky,
I'm sorry you don't have a quiet life.
Who takes away your good life?
Travelers rush by,

Including myself sitting in the plane
Under a busy night sky.

8-11-2000

Identity

It is strange, very strange.
Is this "identity"?
I'm looking for American faces in a foreign country.

I didn't see Americans as special or precious,
When I was in the U.S.
As a matter of fact, I was always looking for other
Asians when I was back in America.

"Mom look, they are Asian,"
I would say to Mom
Whenever I saw Oriental faces.
My dad and mom are from Taiwan.
I thought they would be happy to see familiar-looking faces.
I also felt a sense of familiarity.

Although I am a citizen of the U.S.
Who was born in America,
I have Chinese in my blood.

It is strange, very strange.
I am now surrounded by all Asians
While I'm visiting Taiwan.
But I'm looking for Caucasians.

There are a few.
Who knows if they are Europeans, Canadians or Australians?
In my mind, I imagine:
They are all Americans.

Is this called "identity" or not?
I'm always looking for someone
Who reflects me.

8-20-2000

A Scenario is Playing Out

I'm sitting in a roadside restaurant,
In Taipei,
With a few Chinese dishes before me.
I see cars pass by,
As well as passersby.

Loud voices echo out in the street.
The restaurant owner stretches
Her neck out to see.
Something is happening.
Two cabbies are violently arguing.

The owner said,
"C'mon lady, get out of that cab."
She is talking about what
The cabbies are fighting over:
A confused passenger.

The young woman is crying in one of the cabs.
She is confused which one is the right cab
Since two stopped when she raised up her hand.

Poor lady, she is shocked.
She forgets to step out of the cab
"C'mon lady, get out of that cab,"
The restaurant owner shouts.

I hope this mix-up gets straightened out.
What a scenario is playing out.

8-20-2000
-a street scene in Taiwan

A Bus Ride

You need a special skill
To ride buses in Taiwan.
They don't stop at the right spot.
You have to run.

Prepare exact change in your hand.
Learn to read Chinese characters if you can.
Sometimes you pay the fare as you get on.
Sometimes you do it when you get off.
It depends on the sign above the driver.

The bus jolts.
The bus hops.
The bus goes very fast.
At first,
You may get nervous.
Then you will enjoy it.

The bus keeps you awake.
Make sure you hold on tight,
And sit up straight.
And you'd better
Know your way.

8-25-2000

Misbehavior

I see an American on the bus.
He is white,
Not very young, about in his thirties.
My heart pumps.
He must be drunk.
As he gets on the bus he wobbles
Then he mumbles in the backseat.

"Young lady, let's be friends."
He is talking to the young woman
Sitting next to him.

"I'm a rich man from Texas.
I came here to find someone.
I can no longer stand the lonely nights."

I hear no response.
The young lady's expression is blank.
I hope the lady doesn't understand him.
I feel ashamed seeing an American behave
Like that.

8-25-2000

A Good American

I hear someone speaking English.
A young black man who sits on the same bus with me.
Here we go; someone speaks a language I know.

He looks fine and dresses well.
Politely, he converses with a young lady.
The lady gets off before him.

"Hi, I speak English. I'm from America,"
I say, happy to open up.
The young man gladly speaks with me.
I'm too excited to remember what he's said.
He is an American is all I remember.
A little while later, we say good-bye
As he gets off.
I'm glad I've met a good American.

8-26-2000

Queen Latifah Show

I'm in a TV studio.
This is my first time.
My sister Jessie got the tickets
To watch a Queen Latifah show.

I would rather see Oprah
If I had a choice.
But I am content.
My sister already did the best she could.

At 221 on 26th Street in New York City,
A huge elevator carried us up to the third floor
After waiting in a holding room and a long line outside.

The minute we entered the purple-colored studio room,
We forgot about the cold weather outside.
The audience was entertained by a comedian before the taping started.

The show's topic is about curses of beauty for ladies.
Three gorgeous young women boast about their beauty.
The audience reacts and comments on the ladies.
Some don't care for their attitudes.
Some laugh at their emptiness.
I personally care only for inner beauty.

One hour quickly passed by
Before we said good-bye.
We came away with a fun time
And special memory in mind.

12-14-2000

A Special Gift from New York City

Dad's terrified eyes stared outside,
As if he had just seen a ghost passing by.
My sister Jessie followed Dad's eyes.
She jerked up from her restaurant seat
And ran outside.

Dad followed her out onto the street.
A tow truck was towing our car
Away down the street.

The truck didn't hear Dad and Jessie's scream.
It went away with our old "buddy" (the car).

Dad and Jessie returned to their seats.
Searching for a way
To get it back after eating.

Jessie said, this is New York City;
Once in a while
You get a special gift like this.

7-26-2000

How can New York City Treat Us This Way?

Dad, Mom and I come to New York City
In the rain.
We don't mind.
To be able to see Jessie
And have the whole family together
Is worth the trouble traveling in this weather.

But how can New York City treat us this way?
While we are eating dinner at a restaurant,
Our car is towed away.

Jessie hops into a taxi with us
All the way to 38th St. and 12th Ave.
Where our car is being held.
Even though we are soaking wet
We're happy to see our "buddy" again.

How can New York City treat us this way
In the rain?

7-26-2000

Dream Trip is About to Come True

Dear God,
My dream to go to Greece
Is about to come true,
If you help.

First,
I need good weather.
Second,
I need good health.
Third,
Please make sure grandpa is doing well.

Mom has planned to go to Greece,
And Italy is included, with Renaissance Cruises.
How nice this is going to be
If everything goes
The way it should.

Another nice thing
Is that Dad is coming along.
It seems so unlikely,
Because Dad rarely takes vacation.
He is always busy with his patients.

So dear Lord,
I need your help.
I need a good weather,
Good health,
And please watch over Grandpa
So Dad, Mom and I can travel worry-free.

I'm longing for the opportunity
To visit Greece.
It's an extra gift that
Italy is also included.

12-12-2000

Blizzard of 2000

The year 2000 has certainly been an exciting one;
Before it slips into history,
It dumps a foot of snow on the street.

I don't mind the snow.
It is soft and beautiful,
Like a huge wool blanket covering the earth's cradle.

At this moment
Thinking of travelers on the road,
I pray for their safety, hope they
Slowly proceed to where they want to be.

Tomorrow Dad, Mom and I will be on our way to Europe.
I wish the sky, the road conditions and the airport runways
Will be all cleared up and settled.

The year 2000 has certainly been an exciting one.
Dumping a foot of snow to say farewell,
Indeed, is incredible.

12-30-2000

Every Day Life

A Lonesome Poet

Deep in his eyes, I saw disappointment.
Deep in his soul, I saw sadness.
He is a poet
I met at Barnes and Noble, at
A poetry reading at the bookstore.
Not many people came.
Only Mom, the hostess, the poet and I.

The lonesome poet read his poems with melancholy.
Passion of a past love flowed out as a sad song.
I enjoyed his bilingual poems, Spanish and English songs.
He sang them with his sensitive heart.
My tears slowly welled up;
They almost rolled out.

Oh, unknown poet,
I hope you find
Your true love.

6-27-2000

Please Come

"Please come," the lady said,
As Mom and I walked by a boutique shop.

Mom and I had a little time
Before the appointment with my doctor nearby.
"Please come," the lady said again.
"My shop will be closed for good on Friday,
Everything has to go."

I felt sorry for the lady and asked Mom
If we could help out.
Mom agreed.
The next day we visited her and checked the shop out.
What a nice selection she had in her little boutique shop!

Mom bought me a lot of clothes,
As well as some for herself.
She was happy about the opportunity.
For I never showed an interest in shopping.
Maybe it was time for her to get me something special.
Helping the lady was also something fulfilling.

"Please come," the lady said
As Mom and I walked by.
I wish her good luck
With all my heart.

6-27-2000

Two Dollars

"Two dollars," Dominick held on the dollar bills
And called out.

He wanted to give Mom and I that two dollars
He thought he owed us from last time.

Dominick and his wife Teresa were on our
"Meals On the Wheels" volunteer program list.
Mom and I had been seeing them
For about three months on a weekly basis.

I love Teresa; she is a small, friendly Italian lady
Only as tall as my waistline.
Both Teresa and Dominick are very old.
Must be about eighty-something years old.

Each time when we come,
Teresa opens the door
And welcomes us with her friendly smile.
She holds my hands as she smiles.
She likes me, I can tell.

"Two dollars," Dominick held the dollar bills
And called out one last time.
Mom and I told him, no dollars were needed
For a good meal.

Dominick wouldn't give up.
He wanted to give us his dollars.

Teresa urged us to take it this time.
I walked over where Dominick was standing,

In their living room.
Dominick leaned on a crutch,
His hands were slightly shaking
While he handed me the bills.
"Thank you," they both said to me.

I'm going to miss them very much
When I take a break.
My own grandfather is ill and
I'm going away to see him in another country.

God bless them, the old.
Especially Teresa and Dominick.
They are such a wonderful couple.

8-07-2000

Flat Tire

"Sss…" I heard the hiss coming out from the rear tire.
"Mom, we have a flat tire," I said
As I sank into my seat.

Mom found a big nail in the rear tire
On the passenger's side.
We drove to the nearest gasoline station
To see if someone could fix what was inside.

Luckily, an attendant there gave us a hand.
He replaced the bad tire with a spare
From the trunk.

I said a prayer and thanked the Lord.
Hoping tomorrow, Mom and I
Will be able to get on the road.

7-2-2000

Without A Doubt

God arranged angels to help out,
Whenever to Him we cried out.

Our car tires were in poor condition
For the air was out.

We couldn't stand seeing senior citizens
Go through lunchtime without.
So to Him, we cried out.

Precious Mrs. Liu is a godsend.
She came over and did the volunteer work
With Mom and I quickly within an hour—
Just about.

Whenever we cry out,
The Lord helps.
Without a doubt.

7-3-2000

Nothing Much Nothing Big

Having a good life is as simple as this,
Nothing much, nothing big.

While waiting for the car tires to be fixed,
Mom and I browsed around in a shopping strip.

A boom box played reggae
Very loud onto the street.
I started dancing to the beat.
Mom followed.
She could not resist.

Our happiness manifested quite a bit.
A man looked at us and smiled big.

Having a good life is as simple as this,
Nothing much, nothing big.

7-3-2000

Get Out and Use Your Feet

Behind Mom and I a Mercedes-Benz pulls up.
We are on our daily walking route,
In a new development of our neighborhood.

The speed of the Mercedes is as slow as on foot.
I get a chance to glance
Inside the car behind the wheels
I see a big middle-aged gentleman and a woman.
Looks like they are driving around, looking for a new house.

I gently whisper out with my heart,
"Get out to use your feet.
It's good exercise,
And it will benefit your heart."

Mom looks at me.
She must be thinking
The same thing
For she is smiling at me.

7-9-2000

Noisy Chair

A noisy chair
Cheers me up with its air.
Whenever I sit on it by the kitchen table,
It gives me a funny sound.

Good morning, chair.
Do you enjoy
The morning sunlight
And the fragrance
In the air?

Good afternoon.
Nice to see you chair.
I'm sorry by accident
That I dropped the watermelon on you
Do you mind if we share?

Good evening, my dear chair.
Do you hear the prayers that
Dad, Mom, and I've just shared?
It's been a long day,
We're grateful that
The Lord has carried us through another day.

Time is late now, my sweet, sweet chair.
Cheer me up again tomorrow
With your air.

7-5-2000

Autumn Terrace

Autumn Terrace sits up on a hill.
From there
Rows and rows of cornfield stretch out.

"Look Mom, Autumn Terrace is up ahead,"
I say, pointing to a sign.
Mom and I walk around in
This new development in town.

Mom looks up.
Her face fills with sunshine.

From the Autumn Terrace hill, looking down,
A Jennifer Drive can be found
In the distance beyond.
One of our family friends, Dr. Lin,
Used to live right around there.

I'm not sure I'm fond of my name
Being put up on a street sign.
But I certainly feel great
Seeing my Mom's name up there.

7-9-2000

You Have Nothing On

It was eye-catching.
Three nude manikins
Stood inside a display window.

It was eye-catching.
The three nude manikins staring at us
As we zoomed through the main street in town.

"What's going on?"
This is a very nice town
With many elegant shops around.

"Honey, relax. A big sale is going on."
Mom reminded me. "Didn't you see that sale sign?"

I didn't notice the sign.
But I'm sorry that
The store is going out of business.
And probably most of the clothes
Had already been sold out.

The three manikins had nothing on.
Their clothes were already sold.
I should be more sensitive.
I'm sorry manikins.

7-23-2000

Reliving The Wars

Loud noise came from beyond the woods,
While Mom and I took a walk around the neighborhood
Last night.

"What is that? Sounded so much like a war-zone bombing,"
As Mom said, she frowned.

"I know what it is. There is a concert going on
At the PNC Bank Arts Center," I said.

I agreed with Mom;
It did sound like a bombing.
I wondered how our neighbors stand it;
Especially on a peaceful night like this.

Next to the PNC Bank Art Center,
Stood the Vietnam Memorial Hall;
Many service men and women's names
Were engraved into a round, marble wall,
Smooth as a mirror.

I'm sorry that these men and women have to relive the war.
Where is the respect for them?
And how much more their souls have to suffer?

7-29-2000

Left Hand too

I want to ask the Lord
Not only to hold my right hand,
But my left hand too.

My left hand got caught
Between car doors.
It turned blue and purple.
It hurt!

Mom drove me home immediately
From the school parking lot
Where my hand got caught.

Mom called Dad to consult,
He suggested taking one Tylenol.
I applied hydrogen peroxide on it
While Mom was on the phone.

After the situation was settled,
Mom and I read the Bible together.
When we read about how the Lord
Will hold our right hands,
I quickly said to Him,
"Dear Lord, hold my left hand too."

8-1-2000

Dad is Home

Daddy is home.
A car coming from the street,
Slowly turns onto the driveway.
The gentleman waves his hand,
As he turns.

A little girl, about three years old,
Stands by the garage door.
"Daddy, Daddy," she calls out excitedly.

After her daddy carefully stops the car,
The little girl climbs up inside, through the open door
And up on her daddy's lap.

I wonder if they noticed me as I watched them
With admiration.
I don't remember I had that.
Dad has always been busy
With his patients.

It's okay that I don't have that.
Love can be in different forms
And different ways.

Anyway, I just shared one
By looking at others—a father and a daughter.
Which is not too bad.

8-01-2000

The House of Coffee

The House of Coffee in the Galleria, Red Bank
Is a popular place for young people at night;
My sister Jessie used to hang out here a lot.

I know the place from my sister;
But I'd never come here.
Today I visit the place with my mom;
I'm excited, although I may look calm.

Look around:
Old brick walls, brass antique chandeliers,
Books on the shelves, willow baskets and
Coffee beans in sacks...
It's cozy, classy, yet exhilarating.

Mom and I step up on the balcony;
We pick a small round table by the window.
One ice cappuccino and coffee
I set myself free with uplifted spirit.

Although I've never hung out,
It's really nice to just get out.

6-27-2000

Seven Hills of Istanbul

I've come to the country of Turkey;
Entering an exotic place where
Water pitchers, silver vases
And Persian rugs are displayed.

I'm in a restaurant called Seven Hills of Istanbul
In Highlands, New Jersey.
Great food is served:
Lamb, beef, chicken, eggplant, green, red peppers...
Everything except pork.

No pork—it doesn't matter;
As long as the food is great and the place is exotic.
I see no camels, but It is okay;
I will
When I one day visit the place- Turkey.

7-3-2000

A New Diner

A new diner has opened up;
Mom and I pay a prompt visit.

Inside the new diner,
Brightness and sparkles
Dance in each corner.

Marble floors and mirror panels,
Plus hand-carved glass doors;
Modern moon-shaped lights
Hang down from above,
As though many moons are watching us
From a beautifully lit sky.

A mother and daughter look-alike duo
Sit at a table;
A group of happy seniors chuckle
With one another;
A family with dad, mom, and
Two young sons,
Happily eat their burgers and fries.

Mom and I watch the decoration
And the people inside;
We're holding the menus,
But haven't yet decided.

A young Mexican worker catches my eyes;
He works nonstop—polishing the glass doors
To the countertops.

I'm glad to be in a new diner,
And I make a wish that
The owner and the worker
And all its patrons live their lives
To the fullest.

7-13-2000

The Whole Place is Ours

Isn't it nice that the whole place is ours?
Mom and I are in a restaurant in Red Bank, New Jersey
And the whole place is ours.

All waiters and waitresses serve only
Mom and me,
No other customers around.
Now is a weird hour,
Between noon and dusk.
The lunch time customers all have
Returned to work.

The restaurant caught my eye,
Last time when we passed by.
A romantic outdoor café
Was set up in front of the place.
I liked the café,
And I liked the name "Buona Sera".

Today
Mom and I walk in;
The host leads us to our seat.
It is quiet;
The whole place is ours.

Floor- to- ceiling windows,
With grapevines crawling over;
A theater-like balcony hovers over the dinning hall;
Vincent Van Gogh's painting decorates one wall,
And two gigantic Italian vases stand tall
On the platforms of the other wall.

It's so nice and wonderful that
The whole place is ours.

7-18-2001

Kids Everywhere

Kids are everywhere:
In pet shops,
In animal shelters,
In McDonald's and
In a mother's carriage.

Big eyes glued onto the windows:
"Look, pythons. Where are their heads?"
One kid, about seven or eight, exclaimed.
"Wow, geckos," a few young brothers got excited
When a shopkeeper picked a few of the geckos up
And put them into plastic bags.
Standing by their sides the boys' mother watched her kids
With a big smile across her face.

"Meow, Meow, Meow…Bite the mouse,"
A little girl dangled a toy mouse
In front of a few cats in the animal shelter,
While her little brother cuddled one in his arms.
I knew they would bring one home today
Because their mother was signing an agreement
Over the reception counter.
Good luck cat, and good luck to the happy brother and sister.

"Mom, I want more burgers," the little boy pleaded.
"No, Matthew you had enough," his mother said.
Whaa—Matthew began to wail.
Oh well, Matthew is just a kid.

Now, there was an angel baby in the carriage
With rosy chubby cheeks.
Oh angel baby, the happy one,

Were you seeing the beautiful things around
While your mother strolled you down the mall?

Kids are everywhere ;
They are heavenly creations and fun.

11-21-2000

Today, Today, Today

"Today," Mark said earnestly.
Mark was one of the fitness center trainers.
Mom and I came to visit the newly opened facility
On the recommendation of a friend.

"Today," Mark said again.
As he said it he looked straight into Mom's eyes,
As well as mine.
"If you signed up today with me, you will get a good discount.
But it is only for today."
There he went again.

"Mark, do you mind showing us around before talking us into a
    commitment?" Mom said with politeness.

Mark did.
The facility was huge—
At least a hundred gym machines all lined up in one room.
A four-lane pool,
A Jacuzzi,
And a sauna in the women's locker room.

"So, are you signing up today?" Mark repeated,
"Only today, today you get a special discount,"
Now he was anxious.

Mom shook her head gently and smiled.
As we walked away from the center,
Mom and I simultaneously mimicked Mark.
"Today, today, today…" We laughed all the way
Till our sides split.

11-24-2000

Didn't I Know Him

Didn't I know him?
A familiar face popped into my eyes.

Didn't I know him?
The man worked behind the seafood counter.
He was concentrating,
Putting the shrimp cocktails onto shaved ice.

"Don't we know him?" I asked Mom.
"He looks familiar," Mom said, her eyes following mine.

The man looked Filipino,
With a swarthy complexion.
Something hit me,
Now I remembered.

Max was a one-on-one assistant nurse at hospital.
He helped me when I threw up;
He also accompanied me
When I was taking walks around the hospital.
His job was to prevent me from harming myself;
For I was suicidal.

"Hi," now he saw us.
"How are you?" three of us said it almost simultaneously.
"I'm glad you are doing alright. You look fine,"
Max happily called out from behind the counter
With a big smile.

Apparently, Max had a second job at the supermarket
Besides the hospital.

I thanked him for what he did for me;
And I wished him well.

11-26-2000

No Money, No Honey

"No money, no honey," Tim said.
Tim was a used car dealer.
I didn't know him;
But he was young and friendly.

I came to the dealer with Dad and Mom
Because we were selling off our eight-year-old Honda Accord.
Here I met Tim, a jolly young man.

"Zoom, I got to ride a BMW,
Another zoom, I got to ride a Lexus,
Zoom again, I got to ride a Mercedes-Benz."
Tim excitedly described his job.
Very obviously, he loved what he was doing.

"Jen, what are you majoring in?" Tim asked me.
"Education," I said to him.
"Wonderful, I used to teach too;
But no money, no honey."

To Tim, honey stood for a lovely wife.
No wonder Tim was working hard
To make money to marry a honey.

11-22-2000

Appendix - Depression

A Scapegoat

I was talking to an old man in the next room.
He was beating, kicking, and screaming that
A loved one has tortured herself with the lost of reality.

I'm not sure whose house he went to
But he was definitely lonely.
He needed a friend.

And I thought how could I spend my life
Being sheltered?
Am I a scapegoat?

4-16-2000
-Jen wrote this in the psychiatric ward.
In reality, the old man was a woman.

I Don't Deserve to Live

I was a scapegoat during my early high school years.
I still am.
So what am I doing here?
No one likes me.
Men only wanted sex,
But I wouldn't give it to them.

Men think they can take control of my life.
I don't deserve to live.
Why should I?

4-15-2000

I've Missed Out a Lot of Things

Time has passed and I have missed out a lot of things. Why do I have to live?

4-15-2000

I am Fidgety

I am fidgety,
I have been spoiled and sheltered all my life.
But I don't act like that,
Do I ?

4-15-2000

Hair

Hair, hair, hair…
I have too much hair.
I don't know how to manage it.
I wanted to give it away
To people who don't have hair.
What is my loss could be someone else's gain.

4-14-2000

Bye-Bye Right Hand

Hi, hi, hi…
Bye, bye, bye…

I'm a child within this person.
I'm a child who has been free from writing until now.

My older hand had all the credits of writing;
But not me.
She is resting now to recover from an unknown virus.

I can write,
Not well,
But I can write.

4-14-2000
-Jen wrote this with her left hand.

I am a Ghost

I am a ghost,
No longer a human but a psychotic person.
Does it look like I'm happy anymore?
Right after you have taken my heart away from me?

I am a shadow in the trees,
I am a part of nature being untouched.
I am sorry for not being caring,
But I feel like I'm being used beyond recognition.

If I belong to the grave than be married to you,
And bear your sons or daughters or grandkids,
There will be none.

You can execute me with your sword
And live life like you want to live it.
But I guess, it will never be the same.

4-11-2000

What is It About Being Beautiful?

What is the meaning of being beautiful?
Is it just physical beauty or is it from within?
We are all beautiful in many different ways.
Some of us know how to use it in positive ways;
Some negative.
And others like myself don't know shit about it.
But anyway appreciate your beauty,
But remember don't be vain about it.

4-10-2000

Sex, Sexy

Sex, what is the meaning of sex?
Is it just portrayed in Playboy or Playgirl magazines?
I know that I have heard that in order to be sexy,
You have to look at yourself in the mirror,
And say, "You're a lovely person."

4-10-2000

Being Ill

Being ill is not a grand thing to go through,
Especially on a rainy day.
You have to take medicine for all different body ailments.
Stay in bed just praying to get better and move around.

When something is inside, like germs in wet saliva
Wants to get out, let it out, it's okay.
But do it someplace where people don't have to be disgusted by it.

4-6-2000

A Knife

I feel an invisible knife pierce right through me.
Can it be a sign that tells me I'm doing something wrong?
Or maybe I have missed something?

4-5-2000

A Rock

She is solid as a rock
Having no feelings whatsoever.
Talk to her,
If she can't open up,
Entertain her and make her laugh.

What if she still doesn't respond?
Feed her.
What now?
You've tried everything to please her.
Just say a love prayer for her
And she will be okay.

3-31-2000

Who is Myself?

Who is myself?
Is she a mirror image of me?
What is she thinking about inside and out?
Is she here for an unknown purpose?
Can she go back to heaven where there is no pain or suffering?

4-1-2000

I'm Left at a Grave Site

I'm good as dead being left at a grave site.
Life can be so depressing at times.
Why is everybody so happy?
Can it be that they found love?

I happen to like loneliness as my company.
It is like walking in the desert
As a person thirsting for water and
A will to live in peace.

3-26-2000

0-595-21105-4